North by South

For Marilyn and Ceri

John Davies
North by South

New and Selected Poems

seren

Seren is the book imprint of
Poetry Wales Press Ltd
Nolton Street, Bridgend, Wales
www.seren-books.com

ISBN 1-85411-325-9

A CIP record for this title is available from the British Library.

The publisher acknowledges the financial assistance
of the Arts Council of Wales

Printed in Palatino by Bell & Bain, Glasgow

Cover: Layered feather neckpiece by Anna Lewis,
 photographed by the designer. annalewis.jewellery@virgin.net

CONTENTS

from FLIGHT PATTERNS

from DIRT ROADS

NEW POEMS

from AT THE EDGE OF TOWN

Picture Time

And here's a picture of Gareth's new girl at last,
eyes like bees emerging from a golden hive.
Black gloves; cigarette holder. We're aghast
with admiration, and "You next, boy!" we tell him,
shuffling the pack, fast-dealing him a wife.

Then someone's kids shine out like bells
ringing their laughter through that day beyond
to us. Persuaded by what innocence foretells,
we find "poor Arthur" next, embarrassing; silence
as, carefully, he's helped from hand to hand.

I like this picture of Marilyn beaming widely,
hair brimming from a wide-brimmed hat.
There are my parents. Janet. Dr. Tom. I see
people focused, pinned down almost by each clear
truth yet, without moving, swerving to evade it.

That was Hywel's wedding-day then, a golden fuss,
when the sun came out like a bold, cheerful man
raising his hat, and we waved, and all of us
made almost each of us quite sure, for once,
just what we were – ex-islands now become the main.

What's left for us are these much-fancied traces.
We sit here, all together now, watching them trot
between us, running again through their paces.
Between us, though, they are: reflections of ourselves
that could have frozen us in isolation, and did not.

Sunny Prestatyn

Each day I see them carefully grow old and feed
        behind that glass, those plants,
in an aquarium's stillness – saw at first their need
        for aloneness like a niche.
It is not a need. Lured by sun-crossed memories
        of August, most have retired
from industrial towns at last to find the sea
        sucked out of reach.

They have left wet streets that flow
        on northern towns like tides,
those separately secret worlds that tow
        forever in their wake
lives bound by the going and returning they inhabit,
        for this quiet place
where silent mornings on the daylight hours sit.
        Here no tide will break.

Some watch the sand, the blank sea stretching out, going
        endlessly nowhere.
Past bungalows, an empty paper bag goes yachting
        down the empty street.
Cars pass; seagulls stream on white safaris to the sea.
        Like their bungalows,
the old here are detached, with no shared memory
        to sift or curse or greet.

And if they had known of this, would they have stayed
        where home and friends
still were, where the family once was, and made
        the most of their discharge?
Anywhere, lack of interest, change and age itself condemn
        them, left on some beach
or trapped in tanks. We are accused of them
        and they are us writ large.

How to Write Anglo-Welsh Poetry

It's not too late, I suppose....
You could sound a Last Post or two,
and if you can get away with saying
what's been said, then do.

First, apologise for not being able
to speak Welsh. Go on: apologise.
Being Anglo-*any*thing is really tough;
any gaps you can fill with sighs.

And get some roots, juggle names like
Taliesin and ap Gwilym, weave
A Cymric web. It doesn't matter what
they wrote. Look, let's not be naive.

Now you can go on about the past
being more real than the present –
you've read your early R. S. Thomas,
you know where Welsh Wales went.

Spray place-names around. Caernarfon.
Cwmtwrch. Have, perhaps, a Swansea
sun marooned in Glamorgan's troubled
skies; even the weather's Welsh, see.

But a mining town is best, of course,
for impact, and you'll know what to say
about Valley Characters, the heart's dust
and the rest. Read it all up anyway.

A quick reference to cynghanedd.
always goes down well; girls are cariad;
myth is in; exile, defeat, hills...
almost anything Welsh and sad.

Style now. Nothing fancy: write
all your messages as prose then chop
them up – it's how deeply red and green
they bleed that counts. Right, stop.

That's it, you've finished for now.
Just brush the poems down: dead, fluffed
things but your own almost. Get
them mounted in magazines. Or stuffed.

Barns

Michigan; it is dusk.
We are driving
past big red barns with
farmhouses moored alongside
on a road so flat and
straight it ends in sky,
watching tides of trees
send darkness slowly in
through fences over the pale stubble
to flood the fields and road.
Fading, the barns are almost
all we have by now;
without them, anchored,
where would the horizon be?
It is good to be drifting
near depths of sleep, clear-eyed,
knowing someone else must be
out here where we have
never been before – but not
close enough to tell us so.
Our lights have just
stretched out ahead like arms
and we do not speak.
As the car points into darkness,
I am moving and not moving,
relaxed, unsure where I am,
at home but reaching
at last for what's new.
And since happiness
is a kind of balancing,
then the car and those barns
and the sunken fields
have made me happy now.

For Marilyn

The joy that floating is, on air,
the sense of being everywhere,

the secret of this drifting high
into an endlessness of sky,

is the fixed point from and going to,
the being homeward-bound to you.

Dandelions

Now, they are fleeing downstream, those dandelions
my small daughter has not-quite-thrown:
she raised her arm and let them go, and
the bridge sent its long dark shadow after them.

They flutter around boulders, wriggle, risk
the trees' fingers trailing, as though to justify
not just her casual faith in them but, too,
momentum, what the casually hurrying river's for.

she stands, beckoning at water and dandelions
and the sunlit afternoon. And I cannot tell her why,
now that she wants them back, they are beyond us
both. Useless to explain the river runs one way.

from THE SILENCE IN THE PARK

Mist

mist I have come to like
                    that lets things
        guess what they might be

    the shrubbery's tumbled cumulus
                    not the frozen lake
            a window
                        catching the sun

    outlines leave such space
for what's not there
            to drift astonishingly in

                    that swing back there
                            becoming
                    a trapeze

    the white odour of milk

                through mist also
                    the gate's faint
            harpsichord

Winter

all paths lead
here   curling leisurely
around the lake

or slicing trees
like a skater's traceries
dark on this sudden white
they come
to circle
the bandstand

its worn loudspeakers
are broadcasting snow   more snow
notes falling
to faint applause of trees

the lawns listen
muffled in white

and footprints
fading
murmur
no we have
never
been
here

The Park Elders

the absence in each lap
  cannot be lost
  will not wear out

        in a straight line
        the park benches lean back
        to ponder their own emptiness
        content
                having checked
                    a) the deserted tennis court
                                    playing itself
                    b) more enduring than people
                            the playground's cold iron
                    c) also the lake
                                    exhausted
                        nudging its brownleaf mash

all's as it was
everything is under control

            all they need fear now
                is Spring

A Letter

The poem-as-guest's too polite, so quietly well-bred
that its reticence, you write, is of the dead.

In this quiet place I think again of you and me,
of your single aim. And again blink at your poems warily.

Upon yourself always you turn that desert light;
between the lines I watch you burn, inhumanly bright.

Those you admire all burned and were burned out,
Sexton, Thomas, Plath – springs turned to sudden drought.

Yet to keep a proper space between poetry and their own
scorched selves, what they embraced wasn't theirs alone:

craft that shapes pain into song, the struggle for control
and grace. Our gain's that they sang to sing life whole.

Your frontier's your chosen place and you stay high
where your own space could stare you dry

should you watch too close. I've glimpsed that land
where only self's the mystery, not words, not sand,

and would not want to return though you swear
Nevada would be mine if I'd learn to fly a needle there.

But from reflected heat I learn my own temperature.
This light cooling through trees that moistly stir,

and which seems not always sharp or new, must go
to make metaphors framing what I but half-know

not just about myself till I gradually see it clear.
Evasion, a mere game with rhymes by which to steer,

you'd say – rightly, I think, at times when trees start
shrinking thin to cuttings from my garden. Through art,

eyes may be donated before death makes eyes the same.
True, I need to see more sharp the light you claim

is brightest furthest in. And you, Don –
do not become a ghost town the frontier rolled upon.

So Much

Impressions leap
          open out then drift
as words like parachutes;
          dazed, I can only sift
their clustered fall,
          such a white dense
billowing within that
          Spring seems just coincidence.
So much is happening now.
          Recovered, my daughter plays
in the grass, makes
          cartwheels of her days,
and there's you
          as always on the rise –
my thoughts of you
          are buoyant with surprise
for time which
          bears down everywhere
has brought us such
          flotations on the air
that this seems ours
          too, new-launched sunlight.
Our whole land's
          the geography of flight.
Beneath us stirs the earth,
          above, all branches bow.
I shall write of this.
          So much is happening now.

from THE VISITOR'S BOOK

The Visitor's Book

I

Just where along the line did this voice start
chirping *cheerio* and *chap*, my language
hopping the frontier? Things fall apart,

the sentry cannot hold. Distant, he will keep
barking "Where d'you think you are, boy? On stage?
Back of the gwt!" My cover, see, isn't deep.

My ear/year/here sound suspiciously the same.
Should I say "I'll do it *now*" don't bank on it.
And, upstarts, some new words seem assumed names:

brouhaha sounds like the Tory Hunt tearing fox
-gloves. *Rugger* too. I can't say *Dammit*
or ride phrases trotting on strong fetlocks.

These days, language slouching through me lame
from the States is – well, a whole new ballgame.

II

Cymmer Afan: wet pensioned streets fagged-out
claim only drifting is possible here.
At journey's end, no surge but smoke, no sound
from the deep except some lorry's threshing.

I was towed dreaming on this stretch years back,
a boxed childhood bobbing between high walls.
Then steel's fist pulled the plug on coal
so I was flushed down to Port Talbot.

No, on the whole I don't think I'd go back –
though I do for the usual half-reasons
and took my daughter once. Like me, perhaps
she'd pick up the sonar blips. Nettle-stung,
she proved only the seer's point that one's
Lost Valley is just another's vale of tears.

III

Now big bad Hywel, Giant of Afan,
challenged the far-off giant Mog to fight
then slunk bedwards as his jitters began.

His boots like sheds he'd left outside the house.
Mog knocked. Said Hywel's wife: "Ssh, why frighten
the child" – showing those boots. And Mog turned mouse.

Since then I've known a lot of folk (mostly
non-giants) prop up large gestures at the door,
have thrilled at performances of touch-and-go.
True, shrewd Mog returned later stormily....

But even when your bold front is another's,
chancing your voice instead of giving all
to giant Silence seems best, making close calls
your guests – the art of poetry amongst others.

IV

Thanks to the street-lamp, nightly my bedroom
screens Branches, art on a low budget
restless for review. I give it small notice.
So why a stone-still place I barely know
has been showing in my head for days,
all Valley Gothic and November dusk,
I can't tell. My bronzed brother in America
has yanked such dankness out. At home
in foreign parts ("Shalom, y'all!"), his sights
locked on what's Now like a keen astronaut,
he can never stand repeats. He lives now
west of space. Are old workings still inhabited?
He couldn't give a damn. That's style. Just let
me run these streets through one more time....

V

Cymmer pays out road, it drifts apart.
I'd see him pass then later would learn why,
as a zealous Press damned all "the workshy"
from high ground, that shrewd veteran Dr. Hart
still sends his tall voice across country,
telling how hard at work are the strains
of virus stagnant waters breed where veins
of coal and promise dry up suddenly.

Gone are the flyaway young and the railway.
For the rest, by now all they have come to fit
is too much theirs to detach themselves from it.
Houses, hunched, small-shouldered, face the way
out. The good flat road stretches half-awake
from a life which it steeped whole lives to make.

VI

Dusk. My road shadows the ghost railway track.
Tunnelling homewards, streets smoke twists of string.
I think of Idris Davies who, mists back,
lit up these valleys with poems signalling
the flame must not go out. They kindled each
other, words and people. But old hat, agreed,
and just as well that now he's out of reach.
Who cares which moths on musty clothing feed?

It's nice though that at least a special case
has been made for Viscount Tonypandy's
robes at Cardiff Castle, a special place.
The loyal stockings, too, which warmed his knees,
the wig even, that became his head so well –
how they'll enjoy controlled conditions still.

VII

"Why can't poems be clearer? This one
of yours –." Even now my mother makes me jump.
That afternoon, by car, we tracked sunlight
to hazed terraces where Cymmer tumbled
half in the flustered river, where the house
once ours blinked its bay window modestly.

While she went visiting, I could make out
the road's allusions to stone, obscure trees,
up where it pencilled lines about the heat
on grass. Still I'm unsure just how far
to follow it. We talked of the street
later, those we'd known way back. And briefly
they shimmered in the windscreen, stars
almost there as I took the sky's veiled slack.

VIII

To swerve from village chapel to a town's
high-stepping church is, in midfield caught,
to feel life-forces collide, one woodbrown
and squat, all Welsh (my father must have thought
I'd catch faith like the measles), that tall other
dazzling in a blonde-haired surge of incense
with etiquette's deft sidesteps my mother
introduced me to. Pity, I made no sense
of either. And announcements – usually
in Ostrich – from the pulpit's grandstand failed
to clear up the game's essential mystery.
Even now I am not sure what I've missed.
From bare boards, sudden, to brass altar rail:
it's partly the shock has kept me atheist.

IX

The tv set, stirring itself, confides
in my father in Welsh. Bored, I can see
outside the steelworks signal in the sky
to streets speaking pure industry.

His first language I did not inherit,
a stream my father casually diverted
to Cymmer clean past us all. Brisk shifts
of my mother's tongue worked in my head.

My wife and daughter speak it, strumming
on green places, a running water-beat
beyond me. But though I've picked up some
of the words, they do not sound like mine.
It is like hearing what might have been.
Pointless to mourn that far-off rippling shine.

X

A sonnet's no shape for the geography
of life round here, you say: too cool, too neat
by half for these valleys' buzz and heat.
Hell, you've been reading again, Welsh Disney
stories full of Dai Oddball in a whirr
clean out of his mine, a hwyl-happy freak
down the Con Club proving that plotless weeks
don't happen. I've had him up to here.

As for the landscape, this stretch of valley
narrowed my focus fast. See how the slopes rhyme
mirror-like to the Afan's tidy rhythm?
How everything runs down in symmetry?

No. Well... I've been away too long
to catch the place's rough and ready song.

XI

The *Year of the Castles*, and we are hosts
to flag-makers, tourist boards, sly 'sham ghosts'.
What can castles say to us except that,
once, we were too weak to squeeze them flat?

Its ramparts strolled by slate-capped streets,
an unvisited hill fort became my seat
where over-anxious mist hauled down the hills.
It couldn't stop what is advancing still.
History, we learned, was mostly Royal chaps
and chapesses joined in blurred mishaps.

Well, still their castles stand up anyhow.
And wave. And since my walls are breached, by now
I've had to scratch inside inviolate space
at last for pieces of the starting place.

In Port Talbot

By now it's like returning to a foreign town, especially
at night when the steelworks' odd familiar fever
flushes again faint red on walls and ceilings.
Its reverberations, too, this time I cannot hear
as silence. When cars stop smashing rain to spray
or after a train has dragged its chains across stone floors
what remains is this, work's dying murmur.

Lying flat, the whole town breathes through stacks;
gouts of asthmatic coughing churn the sky.
All night in burnt air, an enormous radio
aglow with coiled circuits, aerials straining high,
blasts out selections from Smoke at ranked streets
with floatings of thick chords that echo for miles.
They drown, almost, the groundswell hum nearby.

Homes of the well-off on Pentyla have the best view
of the steelworks. The main road follows it obediently.
Running coastwards greased by rain, streets skidded,
to this edge, finding metal had replaced the sea
with slabs that rear white-ridged with steam then stop.
All night, rolling in over the beached town
are breakers never seen, a thrumming like memory.

Look out on winter's thin streets. See how steel
lights up the whole town still. Although it shivers now
in November dreaming of steel's breaking point, its people –
kept from clean air but not each other – could tell how
common purpose, gathering, runs strongest
on hardest ground. As here where the land turned
overnight to metal, where smoke blooms in the window.

And when at last shared work's vibrations cease,
sharing itself will fade (as in the mining villages nearby)
with Keir Hardie's dream, with Bethanias long since ghosts,
down history's shaft. Difference and indifference will untie
taut bonds of work that cramp yet forged here a community;
then old South Wales will have to start a New. Meanwhile
reverberations still, slow leavings, long goodbye.

The Bridge

Gareth, this photograph you sent
records August when we met again –
in a city this time like a rocket base.
White clusters judder at the sky.
Our vantage point's a spur of rock
and ahead a bridge, the Golden Gate,
takes off through floes of mist.

I was your second-in-command.
Talking, we watched all afternoon
quick ferry boats pay out the distances
that would always haul them back.
Now that you're at ease in sunlight west
of everywhere, roads you took
return east to Colorado then freeze up.

And we talked of another place,
the bleak hometown ten months before.
Rain rinsed the streets. Our father dead,
we'd gathered in an emptied house
to mourn new space between us all.
Comings, goings, made less sense.
Distance ahead blurred out the focus.

A year from now, ten years, let this bridge
still be there still strung firm
across flotations and coldwater miles,
this connection our father tightened
in a town of steel to show us
the meeting-point survives
and wherever we rediscover it is home.

Moontalk

for Gareth
entranced by his own shining
who walks by his own light and
is all moonshine,

beyond is just blurred mothsville
(my face at its edge perhaps
like a hopeless star)

and he
never looks back even
when wind comes knocking
with white knuckles

young now
he looks forward to becoming
younger a whole luminous
new start

as he talks
through the dark I wonder
again just who the man is
in the moon

and again
whether he ever shares
my occasional unease
about going out

Border Incident

Its churchy reverence for food, those waiters grave
amongst candles, made the place seem empty.
My waiter (André apparently) had passed
the collection plate while I sipped coffee, lingering.
To tip or not? The service had been quiet, fast;
short of loose change, I could always give a blessing.

They were being shown to the table next to mine
as I glanced up. Fiftyish, officer material, good school –
she was in charge, I thought. His was a bald front
of managerial class, a pink all-seeing lens,
as he rearranged his hands before him then sat blunt
at his polished desk, its line of silver pens.

André approached. "Good evening, madam". She bowed
as he passed the menu. "Good evening, s – ".
He peered down, served him an eager stare.
"It's *you*, Mr. Prys-Evans! How are you then?
How are things in Bont?" And he pulled up a chair.
Bald Prys-Evans froze, seemed to count a long slow ten

but "Fine, Jack, fine," replied at last. They chatted
awhile – Jack had left South Wales in '75, I learned –
while the wife's crisp skirt breathed rustling sighs.
As they ordered food, Jack scribbling in biro
on his open palm, I saw her close her eyes.
Three different kinds of wonder watched him go.

The main course came and went and I sat there
riveted. I'd learnt quite a lot about Bont by then,
about bank manager Prys-Evans too, whose steely
wife seemed about to close their joint account for good.
Nodding, he'd suffered all Jack's homesick bonhomie
as if about to explode, knowing he never would.

When they'd gone, as I was leaving at last,
"Nice to see folks from home," I said to Jack.
"Aye, Prys-Evans rules the roost there". He smiled.
"But I fixed his meal all right. See his face
all the time he was eating – drove him wild
I did! Bont, I can't stand the bloody place".

The Engraver

for C.B.

Alone there, some evenings when I call,
you're curved over crisp boxwood,
blades loosing through the strata falls
of shining on landscape's shaken grain.
Paths opened there I'd follow if I could.
Such care, I note, in making light
of blankness; printed then, terrain
you worked streams onto paper and closest
to inked darkness flows the whitest white.

Lines in the night beyond your window
are lumped streets a bulk of sky,
clamped round the lamps, will not let go.
Aerials twitch. Squared shimmers tell
just where transmitted distances run dry.
At home in that block, a boxed space
you have refused to fit too well,
you carve yourself new spaces, unsurprised
by lost blanks in the starting-place.

The view out transcends the frame. By day
at the shop, behind work's stalking-horse
you edge from hedged ground; then away
to criss-crossings of uncommon land.
No buyers wait who'd smooth your course.
What's there though for the taking,
newness through nerve-ends of your hands
keeping us in touch, is here given back
to you for once – a maker making, making.

Carving Oak

Just visible in this oaken bed
the nose and blonde hair
are blurred; I smooth them clean
and set about the rest, a head
sinking (it seems) half-seen.

A straightforward cutting-back
of all I can do without?
Thinking so, I often slip,
miscalculate – then hope slack
accident somehow will grip

what intention meant to do.
And always the dreamt prize ahead:
a face that's more than all
my hopes, that lives right through
them, flickering should I call.

By now, in the grain I can read
too clear the difficulty of keeping
everything I want in sight –
and more, of wanting what I need
enough to get it right, just right.

I think of times when half-mistakes
have smoothed the way: stirring and
blinking up at my surprise, a face
that was always there and makes
its inevitable chosen place

the centre of all my measuring
like a proof to all who dream or
scheme that working, inhabiting a chair,
is mainly to sit in wait for something
surfacing that might take you unawares

and make of your gatherings a prize,
the rhyme that echoes thought exactly
or an image even daylight won't destroy
that you didn't expect, couldn't visualize
and that comes anyway, comes like joy.

For a Small Daughter

With you here, Ceri, even rain's different:
released at last, pushed out on its slide,
each surge down the easy sky is sent
scudding aslant fast to earth on a ride
soon levelled-out. This puddle's surface
is all unseen fish – trembling water runs
away as they dive. They leave no other trace.
Amongst the grass, look, shining buttons.

And I remember, through a splashed pane
earlier, watching swallows tighten the wire,
ready to be aimed straight through the rain
south at a new world somewhere drowsily afire.
Envious, till now I'd forgotten how best changed
perspective is: by our sharing rearranged.

New-born

for Jeff and Chris Crockett

Since just last week
your eyes
have seen through his.
Trust them.
Though your son
can't tell you
what you are seeing yet,
he has begun to share
the true colours of each Now.
Which is not like any other.
You knew that
but had forgotten like us all,
glimpsing things
misted by oversight.
Be prepared then
to be attracted,
not distracted merely,
by dust on sunlit paths of air
or the rooms deep in curved glass,
by rain-rippled windows.
And soon too
(for all newness has its price)
the real earliness of early morn
will be revealed.
Since just last week
your eyes
have seen through his.
As mine have now:
I can see you clear
two thousand miles away
in a new day, newborn.

A Night Out at the Tacoma Dome

well here's a howdy-do
at a soccer match
where the unshy daughter
of a power saw and a laser
performed open-skull surgery
rending the starspangled banner
while the crowd stood still
though pierced from ear to ear
relying on the flag
hands clamped over hearts
protectively
and the flag survived

over-amplified then
an orchestra of muscles:
THUS SPAKE ZARATHUSTRA
drifting of hallelujah smoke
with lightning spikes
and the voice of God
declaiming Laydees an Jentlemen

but just
the Tacoma Stars came
flicking a football like a nervous thought
at the Cleveland Force and
I hope to god
said Gill
they're going
to restore our faith in human
failure
which they did

Taking the Mail to Walla Walla

for Rich

The truck drifts us through this wash
Wallula, Schewana and Wapato leave
in telegraph poles like sunken trees,
the Yakima reservation an empty dusk
and dry except where farm sprinklers
make tepees of light and water.
Now we're delivering bright road
alfalfa flares with the news.

Arms full of wheel, Rich talks
of Frank whose truck this is. Years
of rebounding from Walla Walla to Seattle.
Just two weeks off – Rich's turn now.
Kidneys shot by the jolting, fuelled
by truckstop fats, a mind black-topped
and white-lined.... Frank's *gone* says
Rich whose road isn't sluggish as wax.

At Pasco we unload in the depot's
eerie blaze. Late arrivals sort themselves.
Boxes we pile, highrise of chicks
cheeps false dawn choruses. Coffee.
We push our day through hills of night
that dimly shake their jowls at us
till lamps on the Columbia dams
glitter like swimming pools deserted.

And I think of Frank whom I've never met.
His break from work's become my own,
seven hundred miles of this running
from standing still. Soon we'll be back.
In grey habit Father Familiar looms.
Sometimes though children will point for me
ways clear that Frank must find alone
and no, I would not keep his route.

I tell Rich of the director, United States
Patent Office. He resigned in 1875 or 6 –
there was nothing left to invent.
Rich laughs. Through a dozen jobs
since Vietnam he has tried to keep
his beam full on, I think, and now
through the darkness Walla Walla's coming
like snowflakes, like rustlings in seashells.

McNeil

Beyond talk and laughter
late sunlight
is waterlogged in Puget Sound.
Rooftops also,
embers of this August, show
warmth's struggle
to colour what we are and where.

Out there on the island
McNeil Prison
is a fist on the table.

We are in a house of glass.
As Carl knows best perhaps, his gaze
on the shining water,
a steel hook where a hand once was
gripping his wine glass tight.

                    *

New prisoners leave
from the dock at the edge of town.
Rumbling, the launch stands by
to slip them from their moorings
and heighten what it takes away,
towing them from houses
growing in trees,
the town hall's shameless
white then Mt. Rainier's
pyramid of feathers, a view
growing higher, wider
that McNeil blanks out.

At the scheduled times
the prison's wish
widens
slowly
to a boat,
a beating on bars of water.
The mainland sends it back.

I can see from my bedroom
the island's brain
trained on this drowsy mainland.
It does not sleep.
And when circuits throb so bright
even shuttered eyes glimpse
burnings in stunned space.

*

A power-cut in midwinter.
Puget Sound's gone out.
Earlier, as I read to my daughter
we watched the busy logs
wrap themselves red
and now I am writing this
in a single beam
that shears so much away.
The words are large,
I see myself grow clear.

I should not want things
to stay like this for long.

The White Buffalo

for Murray Morgan

I. Unsettled Ground

Interstate 5 aims up the coast firing cars
straight at Seattle over cold nomadic trails
of tribes and glacial streams, Duwamish,
Nisqually and Puyallup. I drive a steady fifty
where families hauled their lives towards
new ground, hauled them and kept hauling.
On the Oregon trail, with wagons like white
buffalo rumbling west, they left their dead.
And some reached this inland sea where forests
nudged them to the coast, the rivers –
just a few thousands in 1850 – in space
the size of England. They felled, hunted, built,
staked claims to berry crops going waste
they thought. How could they know of the Great Spirit
who'd leaned from the sky to scoop out
Puget Sound and piled up mountains there?

Snow's laid like a tablecloth.
New ground is what I want too. Near Mt. Rainier
we climbed to the one snow pocket so our child
could throw a snowball in July. Fizzing
it flared then we turned into miles of white
as if a single match had set the valley alight,
not even tides of pine could put such whiteness out.

This is another land of ghosts.
Its past is not my own.
Sun bursts on the windscreen.
For now, it blurs unsettled ground that is.

II. The Island

A gull on the pebbles
casts shrewd eyes my way
like a banker asked for a loan.
Its drifting then
is an incredulous slow whistle.
As I cross on a ferry boat
to Whidbey Island, the sun's boom
echoes flat across the water.

At the bookshop, on request
I put out my pipe of peace.
Patkanim would have approved.
He gathered the tribes here,
canoes crisp as axes
splitting water's grain.
They built a fence of seaweed nets
from the beach to Glasgow's farm and,
yelling, trapped their deer. Practice.
A minority of one, Thomas Glasgow
heard the message and departed.
Patkanim hadn't yet been overawed
by the thousands dammed in San Francisco
or earned fifty dollars
for each Indian head delivered.

I am here for a writing workshop
by Robert Bly I leave early.
Thrusting, he is full of the need
to advance, develop, all white
hair on scandinavian overdrive.
The beach puts space back in my head.
Afternoon drifts with the driftwood
and I can forget till the ferry
how mainlands come to meet us.

III. How to Make a Treaty

You find land inhabited by shadows. Having no country,
no history, no flag, they will show you kindness.
Trade with them, your scraps for pelts. They'll gain
your confidence. In time, assembling them,
with promises of presents, appoint leaders for them.
Though you'll have men who speak the shadow tongue,
when your English legalese is read aloud
make sure the translation's in trade jargon.
Whose too few words should keep them in the dark.
And say straight-faced that your Great Father will
look after them – soldiers, lounging, might give them food
for thought. If necessary sign their names yourself.
Later small reservations will dawn on them growing smaller,
marshland or stony upland no doubt, valleys of the shadow.
It is best to seize all rebels before they start to rebel.
Old trails of the shadows will be your highways.
At their edges for ever, shadows. These need not disturb you.
By now you'll have found a country, a history, a flag and
too shown kindness. You will have shown them how it's done.

IV. Doors

They settled near the Green River, three families.
Harvey Jones' land had been a tribal gathering place,
the Brannon homestead strawberry fields
soon to be red again. Returning from Seattle armed
with reassurances, they wouldn't frighten long.
The wells were cleared, vegetables gathered in.
Sunday the doors exploded, showering musket balls
then knives, blood, axes. Mrs Brannon was flung
into her well, the baby too. Three children lived
to tell Seattle had been wrong.

It is out on Auburn Way with my wife and daughter
I hear on the car radio of the twentieth body
found in two years. Women killed by the same hand,
all on the Green River. In Seattle this week
five hundred women marched and sang, folding back
for a while the night. Ground's being fought for still.
Claims, counter-claims and reclamations. A mother held
this sign: *My Daughter – murdered. Attitude – too bad.*
Always the wilderness defeats the settler.
Through thickets of neon, of bars and cheap motels,
someone is moving in.

V. On the Lummi Reservation

Young at the liquor store –
   with a wife and son,
           no job –
     he could recognise
        each eagle in his sky.
   And sat intact,
     patient with me
    who knew no birds,
        with dust and the cars blown
west across America.

   Today back home
   in a gallery
I saw Turner's painting

     'SNOW

    on the welsh

    MOUNTAINS
with an army on the march'

and remembered him.

VI. From Kelly's Diary

December 1855. A cloudy morning
about cold enough to frieze.
The face of the country is not
so broken as that of yesterday.
We see but few Indians.
Our 5 prisners were killed at this place
as they refused to be tied.
Yesterday peu peu Mox Mox
who had come into the Regiment
with a white flag was taken up
by Dr. Shaw and his ears cut of.

The bones of cattle, wagon irons
and 16 graves – they all appear
to have been mad in 1852.
We came upon the Hawkins home with caution
till we saw crows alight.

We have abandoned 3 Mountain Howitzers.
All the Volunteers are ordered
to be mounted that can find horses.
Things will soon be desparate with us.
I cannot conceive why it is
so many youths abandon
their father's house to wander
in distant lands among strangers.

VII. Seattle

Chief Seattle did not fight.
"We may be brothers, after all.
We will see". It was his daughter saw –
Angeline who lived through the 1890s
in a shack on the waterfront –
and her daughter who killed herself.

Now turned bronze, he stares
at the passing cars. In sunlight
September leaves, some new chief's
paperchase through Pioneer Square.
Everywhere cash registers
its joy, and in art galleries

yards of noble redskin hang.
Shadow blurs convergings
it accumulates –
except at the Salvation Army centre
where the light pecks
faces like brown apples pickled.

In 1942 the citizens paid
for a plane they christened *Chief Seattle*.
It gathered a thousand bullet holes.
Then the *Chief* with his crew of ten leapt
the Pacific one more time in 1943
and was never seen again.

Returning, I drive down Chambers Creek
where remains nine thousand years old
have surfaced,
past the sign in managerial white:
Historic Steilacoom
Incorporated 1854.

Cedar logs carved by water
ghost the abandoned beach.
On the skyline, signals
from the Asarco smelter. And I glimpse
also Commencement Bay, whose fish are best
not eaten.

VIII. Leschi Park

The first whites, stumbling, he helped
live off the land. Their treaty ate it.
Then disgorged it fit for visitors
processed as lawn here, encircled
by crackling roads like telephone
lines losing interest in all talk.

Leschi swerved from the reservation.
Fenced off, grass underfoot does not
spring back. His Nisquallies struck Seattle
and though that headline of office blocks
is stern, small print tells how his brother
was killed in the Governor's office.
Bristling, the city's not investing
in the slow business of summer –
bald Sunlight has swept his hat off
but failed to dazzle it with shine.

"Let the whites deal kindly with my people
for the dead are not powerless."
Leschi was hanged. When his band
escaped through the Natchess Pass
they left no trail being ghosts.

IX. Fences

Dad's wandering now.
I built him a high fence –
he'd go in search of Mom
and the dyke's too near.
She died three years back.
Why d'you lock me
in nights, he asks.
Just keeping them Injuns
out, I say.
I call in, fix breakfast.
Jody makes his lunch.

He remembers them
in his orchard every summer,
their old berry-picking ground.
But never heard them go.

My boy's growing up.
Video. Computer games.
Stays in his room mostly.
What with him up there
and Dad in his stockade,
it's me and Jody
trying to keep the lines clear.

I called on him tonight.
Told him I'd fix his radio.
"They weren't *doing*
anything with the land," he says.
And "Is Jody coming over?"

X. Salmon

Boats in the milky morning.
Wind trawls the water,
slow curvings
where white floats wobble.

On the bank
half-circled by pickup trucks
a fire
    whose signals
              rising
    say:
         we have
             retaken
         Chambers
        Creek

XI. Regrouping

As a boy Joe Washington had cigarettes
stubbed on his tongue. Now an old man
at the pow-wow downtown, he speaks
in the common currency. But sings in Salish.
Each winter the Nootcka floods his shack.
Winter again, language of willows pours
downstream on his niece dead, loss
greening loss till sharing sings him home
and the drumming starts, the dancing.

I go outside to smoke.
"We gave tobacco, the whites whisky.
Lung for a liver – fair exchange".
The thrum of hunched drummers is wiped out
by trucks like warehouses sliding east.

Between dances a cop keeps raiding
the microphone. No drinking, check
your children. Holds up a knife he's found.
The watchers, passive or impassive, watch
and I think of a plane crash, survivors
of flung seats stunned who keep regrouping.

This singing in another tongue old anthems
in a shared redoubt, I've no part in.
But am not apart. I have been here before
elsewhere, just visiting from a century
aging faster than time that has said no
to so much now there's just money
as though inside might be someone or
something I'd half-known and lost.

from FLIGHT PATTERNS

Starting Point

Where you started from didn't stop because you left.
Well, no. Hard though to take unflinching
new kinds of doubt you were ever there.
Since the station slumped beyond rescue
way past rails, the river's hauled no hardware.
In clean water, rust keeps coming through.

Expecting patronage – the child you were
the place seemed too, elsewhere made you adult –
it covers tracks, blurs highlights, spreads.
Still, leaves in the playground jump. Sheds leaning
on back lanes forgot to change. Both parents dead,
what but those streets know who you've been?

Once left, the starting place goes soon,
arrives where the road that shrugged you off
chose what's now resolutely called home.
And called home is what you are when slopes pause
for slate roofs to slice a river. Or say honeycombed
workings sag – it's as if new accents echoed yours.

Anywhere, anyway, terraced houses glimpsed
bring in that hill you mean to cross before
it's too late. For difference haunts too, offering
another self to visit, at least a different slant.
But there's a tug. You keep on looking back. Nothing
almost. You were never meant to leave and can't.

Farmland

Inland from the English-speaking sea,
where I lose my bearings and my wife translates,
market towns gather villages.
Henllan, Trefnant, Llanrhaeadr had come
past trees brushing mist from the fields
to Denbigh's plantation of telegraph poles.

Steps stood up, and high arched doors
checking again familiar faces
narrowly took me in. On her aunt's
coffin, flowers had drained the light
but not those packed pews: murmurs, ripples
were refilling farmland's hollows.

The minister's shock of eyebrows
hedging raw cheeks, he'd have hauled a ram.
Speech shook me off. It was tenors
gliding on familiar foreign words in search
of thermals drew me towards the woman
gone, to Joe who doesn't speak Welsh

or often, relying on closed ranks.
Once connection tunes its instruments,
feeling's airborne over fact
and, soaring, forgets it still bears
language asserting difference, how else
leap snags of common ground?

At the coast were fingers of cloud
all bruises and gold rings. Caravans
made one thin road an anywhere.
What we travel from also moves from us,
and gulls guarding clutches of pebbles
turned into people briefly then flew off.

Country

Roaming the airwaves again are rhinestone
cowgirls called Tammy, Loretta, Crystal,
with doomwails of steel guitars.
My wipers blink the blurred road
clear. Even the river nursed in its bed
by sympathetic branches lends an ear.

Heart-stomped, they're stranded
in love's garden. Why though pick late-flowering
philanderers? To be on their wavelength,
I'd need me a Ford pickup and more.
Folk I was raised with kept their griefs
well under wraps, they had no truck
with breakdowns. Would they be leaning on hard
shoulders here, mourning the humped bridge?

But trying to switch off,
my arm does the hesitation waltz.
"Ease up," soft tyres sigh.
"Let go, let go," whisper wipers.

Hymns used to work for them. No road though
runs back, and anyway the songs
aren't all strife. Why not just sag along?
This one's all heart, listen, *Dropkick Me
Jesus Through the Goalposts of Life.*

Pursuit

I've been reading letters my father sent
after D-Day, the edging inland
through Normandy under fire from mosquitoes
then rain, sleep chopped in fragments
("All the guns in France won't wake me")
and, after stand-to, breakfast canned.

"We have come back from the front." Censored,
stray shellfire bursts through anyhow.
A lot's buried. He bathed "in our English Channel",
sang *Lledrod* in an apple orchard.
I'd ask if Collinge made it, Smith,
but all those guns wouldn't wake him now –

and at least one risk made him blunt:
the abbey at Mont St. Michel "is treacherous
without a guide. There are secret passages
so one can easily get lost." *About the front...*
I'd have probed, though we are too slow
to ask the past much, slipping from us.

Still turning the dark side from his family,
he stored the letters in this book he'd keep
safe. He knew us, I think. We knew
the half of him. What he let us see
was the orchard, light cover, you'd have
to guess the dugout seven feet deep.

And I know now that when we let
silence speak it didn't, would not
speak for us, marching to the old tune
Sons and Fathers that we couldn't forget.
So looking at my daughter
suddenly I need to say something but what.

Visiting George

They don't help much, he seems to think,
pursed jowls, concern on stalks. "Do you
remember...?" He doesn't: he'd stood with a gasp
of phrases in his teeth. Then his tongue was there
locked, and he wasn't standing. Slow-lidded
eyes check which effort might call first.

Poured on a small screen, showbiz fizzes.
Will he ask who the rakish Someone is,
selling his new something, bounced off the latest
chat show to this ward? No. Ex-miner, his own light
tilts his head. From here he can see the trees
where flatness holds what watersheds let go.

Back home, that cosh he liberated from a guard
creaks a language living rooms don't speak.
With an ambulance brigade, mouth covered, cloth
disinfectant-soaked, once at a German camp
he saw the known world end but would not talk
of this. "Don't say *I can't*," he'd tell his kids.

So visiting's over. Past trees inching up to green,
Closed signs face permanence, leather jackets keen
on openings. From lanes, the road gathers,
ready to skate way out, trusting in length and luck.
All seems a pause like that note in the camp
diary his son mentioned: "Nobody died today".

Flights

for Rich

Off Route 101 near Spanaway, your father's duck farm
blights an intersection – can't miss it, you said.
Correct. When I slam the car shut, ducks squall back.
Your Dodge isn't here. No one answers the bell.
Out in the rippling field pegged down by sheds,
footsteps have been and gone, it's an ancient
railroad accident, bent roofs, windows cobweb-crazed
over buckets brimming with grass. I peer in,
expect some unhinged Birdman flopped
where only feathers stir. On a table squats his cap.
Overalls look lived in. Chisels curl dry lips.
Dim rows of eggs the local Vietnamese love raw
curve a path back to the house and
you turn up at last, sensation in the duck world.
"You've not missed much. Dad's a mean old guy.
Likes the British though – was over there once."
My road back speeds him out of mind.

*

Three years on and you're coming over,
December. By now I'm unsure who'll arrive
though your letters sound like you, shaking
my breakfast trance back down that year of freeways.

Nostalgic, for once your father's opened up:
you'll find no crime here, land unspoiled.
An eden. His war in England was his happy time
not just for the Thunderbolts he sharpened,
young bloods blown free to a warrior airbase.
Later when airmail letters landed in Spanaway
one by one, mid-table your mother parked them.
But he'd not react. His brother told you this.
Only the fire opened them.

*

You've dragged that damaged thigh up hillsides,
braved black pudding. Careful on stony ground,
we've done the castles. By now we need more space
or less. When you turned up that address
your father explained in code ("Check it out
if you're... Name's Kath") as he glanced elsewhere,
I gladly fetched the map. Dawley's two hours
south-east and it's movement handles distance
so that's how, after misdirections, dead-ends,
this day of frost gone marble blue,
in undergrowth that reclaimed an airbase,
unbarbing wire and sacking the ordnance store,
we send up pigeons to reconnoitre cloud.
In a tunnel your flash-bulb fires rust.
And yellow sweat, look, of varnish still.
Over grassy tarmac around stumps,
our paths converge not only on your father
again where he'd find too little himself.
We fill up winter space, criss-crossing.

Later: "That Kath," you grunt. "She'll be shining
young, still hot for nylons." As we enter Dawley.

*

A good flight back to Washington, you write
of a distance shorter measured in air.
"Gone absolutely British. Bought a special hat
for the feather." Coming from bed dressed
in himself, your father asked so you told him,
expecting him to have known. Yes, went to Dawley.
No, she wasn't there. Silence sent surprise both ways.
"Never seen that sadness in him before."

71

What he'd expected after all those years
wasn't all those years.
Clipped wings in a cluttered field at evening
flare, then settle as trees bank in on the house.

"Anyway, keep writing." Which I will,
for now wondering how that pigeon feather – I took
one too from the base – looks on your special hat.

Howard

In town, a long sad face shunting a rumble
turned into Howard Roberts from Philadelphia
tracking his roots. I owe America.
Tour buses roared, sawing Wales in half
as we talked, and, keen, I showed him our pet castle.
Ghost yawns closing one eye then his other
suggested that belonging might come pricey.

West in thrashed acres where he found
most valleys are depressions between faults,
farms and quarries mourned by sheds
proved rain's not always kind to withered roots.

The bar foamed. Stan folded in laughter, an ancient
head juggling false teeth, a Punch and Judy show.
Howard wasn't unimpressed but shunned groups of more
than one – eyes sad about their wicked weight
of brow turned down his mouth, the grin a wince.
His voice trailing off in search of entrances
or exits said it wasn't a past he needed.

He stayed long enough anyway to lose his tan,
sing with the choir once and leave antique shops
looted. Whole bunches of choice bric
and brac were bedded lovingly for transplant
so though he found not a single root
quite a lot of the old country went with him, you bet.

Mormons

Roads under snapped peaks have eased us
from towns so small their children
glanced up. Sidetracked history rusts cars.
The sun's trailed us through conditioned air
so even from Emigration Canyon
focal points relate: steeples lift
the plain. The faith not ours, ways
people with our names helped make,
glint at desert. Salt Lake City

is a landing place. Those faceless
facing walls: when a big wind shook them,
yes they said to voices calling Jump
that gave them first the Atlantic,
yes to cholera, the Mississippi ocean,
waggons inched a thousand miles into space
under weather's gritted teeth. All slipped land
theirs not their own. And, faith wrapped
around them, keeping the desert out,

received this land. Blown to another world
on prayers, first they had to make it,
the sky striped red then stars flying.
Proposed: we should build as a nation
along the Jordan River with Elizabeth Lewis
as queen. Rejected. But though parched –
two climates merging, heat drains
moisture almost memory – a New Wales breathed.
Sun blinked at the Spanish Fork eisteddfod.

At the university they helped build
are few who can translate them.
Their great-grandchildren who know London
do not know each other. Flight paths converge,
fade out, as sky measures gain and loss.
And soon, welcome as coming here,
our return will give us cloud country again,
pierced by what's beyond, that must keep
changing and not changing to stay intact.

Catfish

We arrived late. He was a friend's uncle, a name
given to spare us one motel, unlucky streaks
of freeway, whose planks leaned on his shack's
wit's end. From a grey head, eyes
gripped where they landed. We answered
in loud British, thrown by his bucking twang.

Just him left with three rooms of the farm grown up
and gone. Work overalls were slumped from a nail
like a taller man, things ploughed and scattered
belonged if they could just remember how.
Supper. He'd be moved soon to the city.
Curtains breathed green as a car unzipped the dark.

Next day, early, when we couldn't see for sun
the smokestacks up ahead, flakes in the shuffle
gleamed as trees panned light. Odd
he'd want us to take his photo. And that catfish
he cooked – we'd watched its mouth open and close
and open how long after the body had been cut off?

Freedom Boulevard

My daughter talked namebrand jeans, the Mall,
as we left the city on 200 West that became one day
without a blush Freedom Boulevard. Bulging in heat,
cars wobbled like toads. Each day she chants in class,
"I pledge allegiance to the flag of the United States..."

The road racing straight ahead, uncoiling sun,
braked in the mining district. You climb past Ephraim
into Wales from the east and it's small,
dry ground's shrunk to a litter of bleached jobs.
Turkey sheds glared into gaps left unexplained.
At the tiny post office, when Mary Davis scanning
my postcard asked if that's Welsh, "No, that's
my writing," I said. *Keep Off* signs peppered testily
with buckshot said connection is accident, that's all.

Sight's longer in dry air: weightless, we fell
like stones on distance whose ripplings
smoothed themselves to a circle with no edges,
the one target that proves anyone's aim true.

The drive-in had *Snow White*. Desert had the darkness,
even the flagged principalities of car dealerships.
Where our block squared its shoulders, the garage
yawned surprise – isn't the point of travel to keep
going? – then shut up.

Snow Rats

Thinking of Idaho, the sky fluttered its dark-browed paleness shut,
heavy with plans, but settled on us. Morning wore afternoon.
We eased out on a crust of light already bushes had grown through,
floating our footprints, pleased with the fat sky sprawled replete.
What to do with it, stare? Not enough, my daughter thought,
nudging from sloth a fluffed plumpness weather sends
for reawakenings. Spades scraped emerald arcs around a tumbledome.

That winter, too, in the river opposite I drowned her pet rat's
ratlets, raw squirming thumbs in a plastic bag. Try stroking Silky,
she'd say, pointing its mad electric head. It hopped humpbacked,
chased by a tail like a fast intestine. My lamplight's circle
shrank. Once when it frisked my leg I yelled, shook her like –

For her, the dome was a kneeling someone to be coaxed or patted up
with promises of buttons, a head. Pride in our created self
lasted two, at most three days then arms slumped in accelerated age.
Eyes sank. In a drained landscape though, fading slowest: the man
gathered from cold, something newmade that is the last to go.

Muskrats meanwhile, whiskery bachelors wedded to prim
                                                        standards,
parted the river when they dived. One sat washing.
She longed to take it home and at that range, well, I could see
her point. She and water took so much in their stride.
Down the river's slide, muskrats on business surfaced not just
in my head and, with her rat at home, it seemed best
(though I never got too close) to go with the flow of her.

Stillwater Blues

We were in the high school band.
I was lead clarinet and he was popular, high
on the fancy outfit, blue with broad gold stripes.
For Don Horowitz nothing second-hand,

guns especially, his dad knew
how to hunt. "It's a real nice day, Don," Mrs. Timms
the doctor's wife said once. "Why don't you
go and kill something?" He did too,

blank sense of humour, charm
fully loaded. When he came home that time, one
of the Few Good Men the Marines dressed fit to kill,
girls waved. He was aimed at Vietnam

the year we built the shopping mart
outside of Stillwater, keeping Dad's business going
when the town was all but dead. Who could tell
things over there would fall apart?

He just dumped himself
is how my father said it. Doped-up in his trailer
a year on, Don sat in overalls, slippers,
on a car seat – a shelf

for all that I could say
to talk him down – staring out everything.
Then he left town jobless and I haven't seen him
since. Until today.

He's killed a man, Don Horowitz.
I see in the *Star* he's Donald Furness now. In the photo,
dazed, he's looking for, what, a job, name (something
beyond him anyway that fits),

and they say he tried to unmake
what this country made of him, threw it all away.
No law against that, feel sorry for him. But hell,
you got to pay for your mistakes.

Say Hello to Phoenix

for Song Ho

1. our lights beat their white wings
   and landed free. cheerfully I greet relatives.

   now is all. buildings have no shadows.

   the Old Man one night near death
   he said What should I be thinking.
   now is here in a suit.

   so many cars. night's driving
   flak that won't burn out. hair of relatives
   on fire – look back and what am I expecting.
   maybe water so calm
   its banks fall through the sky.

   once near Tay Ninh I fished clouds.

   we stop. burnt charcoal after flares.
   now the moon is newcomer too hello
   Moon I am from Ho Chi Minh City.

2. My niece is a bird, get up
   and go. I clean house.
   When she enters,
   my heart stands up.
   Her big American
   makes coffee like ashes.
   One day in the garage wrapped
   in white sheets,
   he was spattered red like the car.
   I said no, no, walked away.

3. I think going measures what returning
   is for, though there is no returning.
   Where are the walkers, old people?
   This is a long street running away.
   When planes come I look up
   and am not here, a head floating.

   I write poems again after work.
   Not storage, remaking, the better rescue
   best if, look, no hands.
   Sometimes there are letters waiting
   with the thought of rain
   but hummingbirds spin and I praise this other
   life that flies through to outlast us.

Driving the Snowy River

It was over, the goodwill season, and even
our tree still switched on in hopes of a second
coming was snuffed by the light of day.
Decorations hung around asking too much.
Why not just write cheques, advised my poems.

Dwindling out of the distance, Jeff called
with that smile on a tight leash. Was it
his job at the bank, some shadow he was born in?
Robust, eating as she drove, maybe Beth
had convinced him life wasn't his natural element.

The river's snow dome swirled.
Trees like ropes strung from branches
striped both banks plumping for low profiles
that panes of ice slid past unbroken.
Against the current, gulls could hang-glide.

Persuading boulders to inch further,
the river surged and though in branched shadow
not one stone seemed to move,
in Utah Lake whole mountains would see
themselves, the art all art thirsts to mirror.

At the bridge when I glanced back.
drifts switched to running my way.
Then trees gave way to hills. Sky rose.
Eyes flew straight where the reeds sighed
over vanishing perspectives, a heron

staring fish into its radius pinioned the lake,
and though even this new season creaked
shining skated me on as if everything
was crushed into one small part of the country
white and only once, this once.

Weeks later, I left the car that had just ridden
rocks into the canyon. Climbed with my wife,
daughter, breathing, and in skidmarked snow
we stopped for our lives to catch us up.
The bent road was going straight

now we'd rebounded, floating on thin air.
Drivers stopped, spoke urgent smoke
but police knew the accidenting season:
welcome back, lucky the river's low.
Home later, why should I stop talking?

Lights at the sharp edge of expectation
coming on like fires burned dinner plates
white, print swerved as a newspaper shook my hand.
On the sports channel: bodybuilders.
My eyes headed south from bunched shoulders

through valleys of the bicep, outcrops
of scalloped leg. When I turned in bed,
strange how my stomach arrived late.
Time for self-discipline, I swore,
self-everything, then failed to sleep.

Next day, remembered musclemen like pet shops
twitched and wriggled. Wife, daughter, offered
selfscapes in proportion. Things levelled off.
But as if to prove heights gained are only canyons
upside down, now the lights came on like lights.

Motel

I got the key
then climbed the metal stairs.

When I opened the door
there was a woman, two small boys.
She asked what had taken
me so long and had I phoned yet.
The two boys
turned back to their tv.

We've been together years.
What if, I wonder sometimes,
I'd opened some other door?

Things to Do When the Town's Closed

Our choir dressed as guerrilla butlers
has driven the holidaymakers back.
It is September. Seagulls
are critics prying over spilt ink.
The town's scraped off its silver lining
to get at the cloud instead.

In search of a bit of life,
Ron has started taxidermy, juggling
bags of skin like a homicidal vet.
They grin from furry cells,
near-squirrels.
You can't keep a good man up.

And Mr. S has emptied his firm's safe.
Self-bloodied, he faked
assault then described the villain
so well for the police photofit,
like a shout his own face rang out.

On the library wall: *ANACKY*.
Draughts from the Mersey Tunnel quicken
across the Dee. Wait,
slow down
at the station.
You can find yourself elsewhere.

Balloons were released in August
from Ffrith Beach for Holiday Fun
with addressed labels. W's returned
all the way from Builth. His prize?
First cash, soon a court appearance:
winds blew north that day so how come W's balloon
went south? Well, live in town
and wind is just a ghost. The label went
via his aunt in Builth, both ways by post.

Yesterday, high on a ladder with acres
to paint, Mr. S was whistling 'Born Free'.
And although the Pleasant Sunday Afternoon Society
now meets all week, although the slipper women
at the laundrette seem lively
and waves roll up in fits watching dunes
fail to outwit caravans,
it's a bad time.

We are alone together.
Even our jeweller's stopped twinkling.
You can't help but feel
someone out there might be planning chainsaw
psychiatry or florist pressing.

Decoys

My timber for carving's from the shore,
driftlumps water sluices out
so it dries fast and won't crack. Elm most of all.
Bones in the woodshed's drought,
they clench. Opened months later, a store
of ripeness surprised is the windfall.

We'd leave for Mostyn, cross
the Shrouds. You had to know the water.
What use is a duck-punt once a week?
You're not informed. Birds on the ebb won't stir,
just sit there packed. The flood brings chaos.
High tide meant hide-and-seek.

I carve birds, ducks often: pintail
and mallard, a teal, shapes wood lays for the hand.
Bandsaw for roughing out – check the grain
runs with the bill. Chisels, rasp. Elm is hard sand.
With oil or polish, what's been fingered stale,
another late surprise, is sunburnt terrain.

Each day – start early. We liked a NE
in the face when we picked our spot:
no wobblings, steady as she... Sixty yards
for a clean kill. 20 ounces. AA shot.
But for food, I wouldn't have killed – at least
not birds. Smooth the feathers, keep no scorecard.

Best I like the curve where crown, cheek,
sweep down through the swell of chest,
the sweptback, cleared-for-action prow
of a poised gathering unrest
that, from the moment's peak,
though wood, might just take off, go anyhow.

It wasn't the birds mainly,
that's something I can't nail.
· *One chap I took, a February morning,*
sang for hours – threats to shoot him failed.
Never sung before. The estuary
was fine, I lived on dusk and dawn.

Beyond wood: an airy something
from nothing wood's a pretext for.
Alone at last with the whole mind's scope,
you drift. Almost a familiar shore.
Stirrings, gleams are stalked, and springing
this time they are yours, you hope.

Wings

Time hadn't mattered till her husband's ran out.
The house, spreading, made an evening of itself.
Reedy flats stretching out to a horse
and banging door for company met roofs on the run
from dunes. Careful, afternoons measured
the estuary where tides weighed logs
then put them down, where hours drowned like clouds.

When the ex-minister, fifties like her, kept calling,
his beard through pipesmoke she read first
as contentment. He had seen the world and shrugged.
Wrong, he had dabbled in property till it bit him.
He'd collect firewood, taking logs for a stroll
in a stripped pram, put up coveys of gulls
brought down as he tracked the shoreline. She saw
not washed-up footprints, water quicken slippery
as wind past the lighthouse, rippling implications.
Ships had been juggled long distance till its arms shrank.

The roof leaked. Mornings he'd spread planks, tools
and disappear. He'd finished the process
of getting started. And would have finished
the job but then the roofing season ended.

Once at dusk when she'd thrown stale bread,
the window floating, floating with white wings
settled on water. Not just perspective though
of the opposite shore kept sea dreams in check.
He wanted to preach again so she fixed up
practices at Bethel, listened from empty pews
and drove him home. Theirs was an oldish house.
The roof seemed shaky but faith might hold it up.

Burying The Waste

Holywell

Trapped by Caradoc, favourite of a king,
even Winifred could not deny his sword.
Where hair leaked blood, a well of healing
sprang, then the stream hurrying its hoard
of news woke up the valley. Winifred
drew pilgrims limping, eager to be whole.
He signed up slaves of cotton, copper, lead.
Her stream, severed by water wheels, rolled
machines. When Winifred spread her arms wide
to make from shadows trees, he cut them down
but she thinned the Dee channel. Its quayside
became silent, the valley a ghost town.
Now buildings sprawl headless. All around,
sprung green, half-buried: still misshapen ground.

*

Not just the Church preferred its blessings high.
This cotton mill snatched six storeys of sky
with stone from the nearby abbey's shell
then, power untapped, St. Winifred's Well.
An act of God, a world in seventy days.
High too squire Pennant's recorded praise:
all the workers flourished, dined on meat,
fish, "in commodious houses". Work was sweet.

Poet Jones of Llanasa, muffled voice
of the backwater – why couldn't he rejoice?
"Rods doom'd to bruise in barb'rous dens of noise
the tender forms of orphan girls and boys."
Poets. They build nothing. Just hover, stare,
write maudlin history. Except he'd worked there.

*

Ingenuity flowers in such fumes.
New copper bolts were roots helping great ships
spread wide. Brass beakers moistening the lips
of Africa, exchanged for slaves, seemed blooms.

Up there, notice, a fly-wheel gouged the wall.
In this bank, too, an opening faced with brick
like an oven gone drowsily rustic:
no grass, webs or wormcasts though. Earth, that's all

almost. Hereabouts being where the knack
of refining human brushes took hold –
twigs bound in rags who carefully swept back
arsenic from this flue and lived to rot –
last year they found a skull, some ten-year-old
ingenuity planted then forgot.

*

The wall keeps on haemorraging dark green
through the bricked-up centuries, through soil
Meadow Mill injected with copper spoil.
And its damp spillway is coloured gangrene
in memory of times, as Pennant said,
when workers obeyed the "antient law"
of sluicing thoroughly before meals or
watched "eruptions of a green colour" spread.
(They knew dogs, if they licked the sheeting, slept
for good.) So justice as well, urbane,
copper-bottomed, is remembered here. Yet
though the wall's washed scrupulously by rain,
strange that metal still heaves through. Dogs drop.
It has tasted men and starves and cannot stop.

*

For three years, Frederick Rolfe alias
Baron Corvo, the Crow, pecked at the shell
of Holywell. He saw in it himself,
more idea than place, a proud man mostly
beak who squabbled, wrote and painted, furious
with "Sewer's End", obscurity's rebel
till fury grew him wings. Two crows he left
in painted banners still caw "Look at me!"

Flashing, art's narrowed gaze will open
on polluted water and turn even stones
to mirrors. The Well running wheels ran men.
Its stream's "uproll and downcarol" Manley
Hopkins sang rang walls from where Poet Jones,
apprenticed to heartache, jumped to sea.

*

Ice tore a trench to the estuary.
Grass healed its sides. Water devised a well.
An idea, grown around it like a tree
surviving as an arched stone spell,
towered so pilgrims are still beckoned here,
a welling of belief that named a town.
When another idea for water
bricked up the flow, its weight wore people down.

The centuries keep waking to change dreams.
Dug from the undergrowth: brickwork's feud
with stone for possession of the stream.

And voices insisting water is alive –
those pursuing always and, pursued,
those in need of miracles to survive.

Barry John

who tacked like a yacht
through breakers,
tidewreck where he'd

been, whose arms, hips,
swapped fly half
-truths tacklers grasped

too late, was a spool
casually unwound
around sharp eyes

lining him up just right.
Then he'd crossed
their lines, parachuted

in, pass master
of the national art,
straightforward veering.

Flight Patterns

Staying, moving. Both versions
claim the coast, illusions

of choice steep
depths here and beyond keep

prompting: packed in redoubts,
hiders watch runners wearing out.

Our hill, to us a giant cast
in rock, eyes at sea sail past.

But nowhere special's lee
is also where ships are mostly

and, although smudged by tides,
here is a lifetime wide.

Sometimes staring at Where again
eases the strain

of Who, looking out there's
safer. Though a lot of who is where.

What's sure is: not enough alive,
waking, I try

to keep in sight
one-off airy sleights

of place as they somehow
light up here and now.

I've inherited what I fit
almost, tried living in not on it.

Still, out there's blur
is mostly the one in here.

Look at swifts, spun
arcs bounced off reflections

of themselves in a rippled place
towards definition none trace

yet seem to aim for, stirred by flares
on water. Thirst here, now, everywhere.

In the absence of belief,
connect sun, look, with that leaf.

And there are sounds
always voicing familiar ground.

Just out of sight, human shapes
are reclaiming wired landscapes:

what's past too
prompts Where's conspiracy with Who,

and should being British strike a chord
I'll know I am abroad

where (though distance lends detachment,
little else is lent)

anyone can go, the knack
is in getting back,

Elsewhere-at-Home no nearer, the one
impossible destination.

from DIRT ROADS

Footprints

O.S. maps are fine except in forestry
where paths breed then forget,
having trees to get to, trees to see.

Each seemed the least travelled by.
They made no difference till one
gave me a shot of field and sky.

Rhiwddolion was not lost. Sprawled
houses measured the distance
between forestry and stone walls

where doorways wide enough to say
"They've gone" had ferns on mantelpieces,
draped boughs of another washday,

flicker on burned-out hearths.
Slate slabs crossed a field
like giant footprints: the one path

still went to chapel, straight.
By the time I left, there was just
that well-heeled shine of slate.

Conifers loomed. Keeping confidence
intact through shadowy twists
and times takes a lot of ignorance.

The Quarry

Out on the ridge,
I checked the incline
to a row of sheds
leaning on each other.
Dead-ends. No sign

but I slid down anyway
past winding gear.
Clear on a wall,
these scratched words:
"I am not here".

Glanced up. That close,
a slate tip collapses
avalanching, stopped
for just seconds
to let feet pass.

Remains of a still-warm
fire could be anyone's,
candle stubs too.
Walkers get everywhere
though I'd passed none.

I checked the shaft,
swam on my feet, eyes
gone, down sides
sucking me through
trickling ricochets

till it split,
it forked, I could feel.
Stopped. Couldn't turn.
Which of us, which
one's the quarry?

A breeze. Light
as if someone yanked
a door then stood
aside. I edged out
on rails. Hacked

slopes. On an upturned
wagon, scrawled,
was "This is not the way"
Move on. Feet
clattered the rockfall.

Sky was a lid.
Walls gathered round,
forcing more stone
down a crammed
mouth in the ground.

I reached the rim,
unplugged my boots
and grass slid me
out through open sky
the fastest route.

Lights, a dream begun
without me. My pack
creaked, bringing
the mountain down.
I said when I got back:

"There's no one there".
It didn't take long
filing my report
Next day I checked it.
Someone had scrawled "Wrong".

Lift That

Tonight I thought of the old man, seventy,
my uncle who worked with his son-in-law
in a dead-end shaft, just them, dragging
slate from the wreckage. Only
twelve years back. It seems a lot more.

Even eating, sometimes when I'd pass
off-duty, they seemed apart. Strange how
sandwiches need watching. The old one
would answer, both say nothing. Partners?
I couldn't believe them, towing

slate on cracked wagons through the gloom
where only water was going on
and on, when the lit town below
had everything. Except workroom.
They were like fossils trying to shed rock.

I know this, it was cold. The old man
called me Sarge. The other bothered me
and, once, I saw him stride from a shaft
with a big green slab in his arms.
He dumped it smack at my uncle's feet.

"Lift that," he said (I'm translating now),
"then criticize. I'll treat her how I please."
It seemed to me the old man hauled
silence mostly. He'd changed. Anyhow,
I didn't go back up there for weeks.

Then, "The young one's gone," someone said.
When I visited my uncle, notebook
shut, at his house dragged from the quarry,
his room had just got out of bed,
tools everywhere, wet clothes, boots.

"Said he was going. Good riddance."
Nor was his daughter, streets away, upset.
That was that. People talk though, even
gossip's checked on the off-chance –
we had to put on a show. I won't forget

our lads strung out in macs, a Wednesday
harvest across half a mile of slate,
rain, slate. It was pointless,
and cold weather put the dogs off. Anyway,
"He'll be home again in weeks, you wait".

Days later, it dawned. Could be. Sweating,
I climbed to the quarry in full kit,
levered that green slab the younger one
had hauled, and started scraping.
Him. It was him. Then I replaced it.

Where You Are

I

For Billy Rice of Blaenau Ffestiniog

What to do with slate or life but shape it?
Carved before your time, in Dyffryn Ogwen
are starbursts in shelves, and birds inhabit
mantelpieces. Now edges curve again:

turned on your homemade lathe, mossgreen,
that bowl slid from bed unbroken. Its base,
rough proof of origin, deepens the sheen
of your part discovery, part rescue.

A zodiac at Tregarth lights a fireplace.
Time shimmers. Folk the art schools never knew
assert what television screens deny
outright: what you have is where you are.
Turn to reflect light from an inner sky.
Find rock shining clear as a lodestar.

II

For Peter Prendergast of Deiniolen

Up on the slope, two boys were ferreting.
What slipped down eager as bad news again
was emptying warrens as I climbed the lane
to your studio, from winter into spring.

The fuse from boyhood's coalscape, underground,
had ignited canvas. Slate country flared
with you, blasts of colour from midair
sparking hollows, in land that seemed newfound.

I had thought such colours too bright. Today
near Llanberis though, from a shaft that turned
ice black then burst on an open spillway,
I saw it, an explosion of wet fern.

Angle of entry is all. The ravine
is dark. I wish you multitudes of green.

Riders, Walkers

Damp, cold, dust? They were for the pack.
For one man in 1939, arriving on horseback
with his company, air conditioning was installed.
Swept slate caverns at Manod became halls
when Charles I, painted by Van Dyck, was stored
out of bombing range with London's hoard.
He looks grand still, unsurprised to be around.
The quarrymen, alas, stay underground.
But in the National Interest, common sense
says things of value must take precedence.
Think of the painting that you value
most. Walkers give way to riders. Which are you?

They had their place in the picture, cold, damp,
for Mary E. Thompson at this time. Cramped
by ill-health, she leant ambition's ladder up as far
as the Brussels Academy but surfaced in Bethesda.
From a split block, a small cloud of dust
escapes; a pencil can feel rock's upthrust.
She walked, climbed, and for almost twenty
years the galleries she toured were quarried,
sheet after sheet, as pale drawn workday
faces against stone in all the colours of grey
defied mass. In time, she could tell them who,
when they asked, pointing, "Pwy 'di'r un acw?"*

So here is Alun Jones, blacksmith, concentrating
down a studious nose. Will Proudley cutting slate.
Here is the art of shaded surfaces, its value
that record sparked revelation. Not high art, true,
but true not low. Part of the story
half-buried still, it redefines nobility –
like the slate bust of Gwilym Hiraethog, icon
of nonconformity detached from the salon
at Penrhyn Castle (and carved by?), firebrand
snuffed by the country of the bland.
In a cluttered glass case: the fate
of art, shown to an antechamber, in an unfree state.

*Who's that one there?

Bikers

At the village with no car park,
slate's lava flow was in place
even of second homes.
A band of conifers sneaked
out over the hill.

All afternoon, the hang-glider
circling like a kite
turned kidnapper had threatened,
unless the place paid
some attention, to let go.

But frames couldn't straighten.
A bad case of extraction's
rictus, how could it look up?

Down the incline hiccuped by ruts,
bickering, two dirt bikes droned,
groping to pick up din.
Then shrilled flat out
through dust barriers smashed in the blast
past sheds, a burnt car –
two of grit's thousands
grinding the crater's edge.

Retake workspace, deny
waste. Take chances not helmets.
Wreckage you're always heading for
and can't fly from
fill roaring with yourself.

Reading the Country

I. Sentences While Remembering

"I'm going to paint," she said, "your portrait".
But turned up proudly apologetic
with this townscape she'd held back from the Tate.
North or south, yes, I recognised it: slicks
of wet slate, where the hills pull up to brood
on drainage, spell out opposites of wealth.
The Welfare. The cafe molesting food.
Stoned houses. Just the chemist's shines with health,
not good, and Bethania, falling apart
since takeaways dawned, offers carpets cheap.
Grey magic. A paintsong sung by heart
to the tune *Doomed Rhapsodies of Sheep*,
it was all mine. She shrugged. "I'll do your head
next," she promised. "You've done it," I said.

II. The Lost Kingdom

"Money," they answered him, the old pair roused
as if by a mansion grown from seed. Young
enough to bend, he tramped farmlight till spined
slopes fattened into valley. A big house
wallowed in shrubbery. He daydreamed. Sprung,
a smoothed passage took him in. Rockshine's
hoard of promises looked damp where he found
there was no door so he tapped, hammered, kept
on, hooded in candlesmoke, heard spellbound
his quarryings harvested. They were swept
to a tinkle of glass on the slate wall's
other side. The wall never thinned. Farmland
dreamed him, under its crown of thorns. A fall
of light late on, showed him his ancient hands.

III. An Old Thing

He'll, listen, wheeze like a busted sofa.
Then that matchbox rustling in his chest
ignites. Jesus. He's his village, depressed,
a quarry worked-out, the last railcar
from Llanberis a century away
from our coastal town, and now he's stopped.
At the old folks' home near the video shop,
he's not dressing or undressing slate today.

It was a war so they slept in barracks,
men against rock. He caught fleas, lost an eye –
not a dry one in the house, all flak
the way he tells it. A life cabin'd, clearly
gone. All that stuff about *cabanau*.
Still, you wish he'd not asked, "What's your story?"

IV. Cwmorthin

It has emptied, that bowl of a valley
hung cracked in Blaenau's draughty rafters, true.
It isn't empty now. Some rework slate.
And the new roads that make all secrets free
send weekend ski jackets glittering through
along paths half a century out of date.

A while back, the mute chapel's disbelief
flared white into graffiti: *Twll din
pob Sais* and FWA. They're fading though.
Trails thicken. It stares like the old chief –
scarfaced, somewhere innocent of wheels
till foraging newcomers cast shadows –
who asked how many, how many more are...?
and the answer was, "Like the stars".

V. The Fisherman

The path tightroped over metal rubbish
fell in a tarn of gleaming liquid slate
more likely to hold fossils than fish.
Eager, he came over to the sluicegate,
young man, rod bouncing as his wet line winked.
And, accent not at home, chatted. Lately
he'd been dabbling. "Any in here, d'you think?"

Right out of luck, work, he deserved this time
better than the truth. It was spring. "Could be,"
I said, and waved as I started to climb.

Near the big house's shell, rhododendrons
bursting their marquee of pines rushed high
up the incline. Rails were rust ladders stunned,
pointing at a quarryful of sky.

VI. Captain John Huws of the *Oriana*

Who? Oh, some ghost here at the marina.
Let's say Davy Jones's locker-cleaner
raised on the local diet of hard rain,
muttering a dying language, Earstrain.
Kill that outboard anyway, get a fix
on lunch. Scramble-up some electronics.

End up as him? Listen, you'd have to be
reefed on sharp memories and all at sea,
give way to God not cabin cruisers, rid
yourself of weekend doldrums, wife and kids,
have sailed tall ships to San Francisco
from Porthmadog or through hell to Rio.

And still be back in time, a bit leaner,
to watch you navigate the marina.

VII. The Weathercock

After Glyndŵr struck, grass sprang in the streets
where deer grazed. Now all that's behind the town
whose quarries are shrouded in forestry.
Ignore the big hotel's recent breakdown,
shops for sale, demented peacocks shrieking
at Llanrwst. But does its castle (occupied)
belong to it or does...? Which tongue to speak?

Difficult. All manoeuvres must be deft.
Hovering, even the bridge can't decide
which is the Conwy's right bank and which left.
No wonder the weathercock's in a twist.
These days it recalls, airing its tall tail,
a favourite son, the one Welsh nationalist
peer of the English realm in all of Wales.

VIII. Barrenness

for Kyffin Williams

Best of all your paintings at Oriel Môn
I liked that figure in a rockscape. Sky's
going one way, the man another (down),
and mountains after him heave black stone,
mad as thunder. He is elderly, spry.
He is about to leave the frame or drown.

Now a trained English eye might take this chap
for Everyman in a painted sermon
on barrenness, all you need ever know.
But names matter: in coat and damp, flat cap,
this is *Dafydd Williams on the mountain.*
It's one moment, place. One life. And for now –
rained on, grimly passing through his portrait
homeward-bound – Dafydd wants out of it.

IX. The Pylon

i.m. R. Williams Parry

It stood up. It flashed, whistled, as your hare
escaped, grass-mirrored streaks. Now pylons
seem (that was the thirties?) local hardware,
suspension bridges between then and now.

Last year near Melynllyn under white-capped
hills you'd know, a pygmy deer played come-gone,
swerved, jumpstopped, became two hares. Somehow
they had earth mapped, crazy with grasslaid traps

as it is. These days, what comes overhead,
that falls and is nowhere everywhere, weighs
heavier. Trees know. And water, lakes stunned
way down by such pourings on clean beds
of impure streams. If you could.... Anyway,
this cannot be swerved from or outrun.

X. The Moment

Way down in the giant bran tub plundered
of its treasure, overburdened ledges
still tipped, painstaking, filling the water.
Dead end. But a boy shuffled to its edge,
leading two flippered divers with their tanks.
Who became, billowing face-down, airmen
with baggy arms and legs outspread, then sank
as their whirlpools parachuted open

to a flooded world. Stone ruins inlaid
with mud. Maybe a tramline broken down,
one truck, its rust-wrapper flaking away.

And one survival: the sound breathing makes
like language under pressure, almost drowned
but strong close up, echoing in their wake.

XI. The Old Language

is yours if your word for home means "here".
Whatever it nudges from retirement,
sharp-eyed, beckons lost worlds words nearer.
It makes more connections than were meant.

Streams clear the throats of derelict caves
to deliver rivers that have outgrown
ruin fluently in slate villages,
in towns that are mills still dressing the flow.
Here is not home and doesn't sound (riches
pour past!) much like my country. But it is.

Echoes outlast sound. Listen, nudged awake,
they too murmur. Says earth's vocabulary
of names on scribbled surfaces, it takes
more than the one tongue to speak a country.

XII. Penmon

for Ieuan Wyn

We left the quarry town still tunnelling.
Roofless, men roofed cities with what they'd found.
What were they looking for? Where the Straits swing
open, it seemed far off, that ripped headland
whose priory also broke new ground.
I'd have your poem translated, I said.

In uncrowded air, a buzzard wavered,
casually tightrope walking. Then flew on
through your language and mine blurred
wordless in the skimming towards Penmon
as if rock's undertow had been washed green
of the faults words still try fathoming, thrown
by the eye over so much space between.
us, so much spanning it, above, below.

XIII. Llyn y Gadair

i.m. T.H. Parry-Williams

Near the freed schoolhouse smoking at Rhyd-ddu,
a slate track still wanders off towards work,
feet thick, over boggy ground. It's a quay
by now: someone has launched into the murk
a Morris Minor where barbed wire, too, dives.
No wonder crowds at Beddgelert choose
a past well-crafted. So little survives,
the plot thins. Why pause? Something though moves.

Not two dry quarries crumbling like snow
on a straggle of thirsty conifers,
nor even the lone fisherman towing
his shoal of ripples round the lake. What stirs:
their belonging, stubborn greys, washed browns,
to a dead man's vision not closed down.

XIV. Bits and Pieces

Why speak of such things? Because, under news
of the airports' pearly culture eased
through opalescent screens, plain voices say
what joins-up hills is more than just the view.
Because hills blur. Now eyes can't see the trees
for Hollywood, crammed ears turn the way
of the jogger soundproofed against spring.

Dead poets, tracks of the quarrymen, lakes
mining silver – why dabble in such things?
Because the living river of them slakes
now with then. Strongest in ground fractured,
it can flow speechless underground, go slack,
and mistrusts most the fluorescent sea.
But it runs on, pulling in the country.

Portmeirion

Cloud has new domes to deliver,
the estuary (when it can stir
itself) water for islands
to be dipped in shine. Stream
slippages show how earth dreams
too, gleams packed in sand

plumped by tides full of elsewhere.
Wings, scattering, assert airy
claims that there's no fixed place
in the curved world's spun
spray of easy transformations.
From the hill, floating them in space,

this village or pastel fountain
spills bright things born again.
And its weather-vane points firmly
everywhere in the play
of light on stone via Fabergé
and Llŷn by way of Italy

that is nowhere, says the piazza's
line of gilded dancers so far
from Siam. Roofs reel. Hereabouts
are follies. This one's riches caught
forever on the wing are the rare sort:
brought in for once, not shipped out.

R.S. Thomas

I

Some comfortable harbour, say,
tugs a boat like its own
from the sea. Moored,
strangeness brings the storm.

Nights flicker.
And there is the manse's attic
blown, one curtain,
a lighthouse marvelling
at the bouncing moon.

II

We stood accused
of reading him. Wrong
language, place, wrong century.
Though his shadows from the fields
match ours, he made his own world,
lashed it for not surviving.
Which way forward but back?
His territory only boulders
gripped like knuckles.
It was shrinking always.
Rage kept him reinforced
until, falling short
of himself in the light
that language cannot span,
he saw a rimless world
extend the gifted heart's idea
of self, which is poetry.

III

Wind in the throes of turning
sighs that we have no centre.
He is our capital of echoes.

Places we find ourselves
not often, store voices far
from aerials turned to base –

one voice can set the whole
wood calling. And one wood asks
how earth and the planets

hang together, trees lit
by a bright field,
mild locals in eternity.

He reaped necessities:
dreams, with slant light
through our crowded sleep.

Our harvest, waking beyond
pylons skewering the hills,
is new land opened.

Mountains, Valleys

These whirled nights, slate
   splashdowns on our lawn
from a darker world, the roof
   straining, recall how long
tight overlapping worked.

Their lichen's spattered
   prints show hands gone under.
But what's buried holds
   things up. Roofs go on,
slates ranked in careless air.

And the tips of excavation's
   bulk of waste near here
still baulk at leverage;
   studding northern green
rollers, they have outlasted

black bergs of the south.
   So much turned inside out
in that other place translated.
   Now it's a job to find
what hasn't been ploughed in,

links gone with the chains,
   where mysterious kings
in childhood's territory
   of blackfaced men
had rearranged the earth.

After coal slid, stopping   ·
   children dead, came levellings.
With closures, tremors
   at slack of night. Fast change
for those settlement gave grip,

pegged to ridged slopes.
   Pressure had fused them,
resisting slippage where soon
   trickles of housing
swelled the teeming coast.

In search of balance,
   mind checks its levels
for sound. Idris Davies'
   songs of the plainspeakers
named their coalscape Wrong.

Pits, slag, each chapel like
   a chapel. Style? "I don't
sell it." Style, though, it is,
   in praise of nouns dug-in,
mobilised by verbs that left,

after London wiped his eyes,
   space between poet, people,
just for his one voice.
   Yet not one only. The upland
he shared with poets, crests

where the sun had supper.
   How to sing high and low?
Hear Shelley, Rhymney, rhyme
   almost as he tried reconciling
earth voices with the sky's.

Alun Lewis above Aberdare,
   strand of a tide swinging
wide towards India,
   would have known of this.
Below, scuttled workings

measured their allotments.
  Feeling two undertows,
his sight peopled, he drifted
  where clarity's white
spread glare of promise

cleared him out. Hills blanked.
  Sun that dried his language
not heart, impaled him on himself
  when, at starvation's camp,
he left fresh bootprints.

Trying passwords still,
  he slipped connection's webbing.
Yet lives: his rescuers,
  those lines of his despatches,
struggle alone tautened.

Hills grazed just by clouds
  keep calling. Outcrops from us,
rooted, facing out, such minds
  answered for themselves.
But were trailed by roofs

where paths to the crests
  best measure distances.
Spreadeagled, the uncommon view
  can blur heart's commonplace.
Closeness though cramps vision.

So what if screens flick instant
  distances, repeat everything
worth anything's brandnew?
  Now that the balancing point
is anywhere – work dispersed

where the wronged rain falls,
   air's quarried or sea thickens –
ranks in the air press houses
   to remember. In shared
climate everyone's the weather.

Sheriff

When silver was found, a few of the boys
got married in the excitement,
wiped out the last Indian
then named the town after him.
The sunlit river beating drums
still has silver going for it.
But spoilheaps yield scrub.

Sheriff's in competition with
his health. A single-barrelled stare
tracks bored teenagers, hormones
on fire, his son might inherit
if he returns from California.
Beyond cars, trails shrug off
the emptied slopes and climb.

The past's hard on this place.
In a shack years back, he found
bleached newsprint turn to Moscow snow:
two German generals marched,
heads unbowed, with beaten troops
as if the shack had to store
a reason for staying upright.

Rock, shimmering, squats in wait.
Sometimes a waterfall of light
pours off a ledge. Its overspill
is his road between Elkhorn and Duchesne
which, though hazed like
anything too near to be in focus,
has veins of pure glitter.

Haze lingers. Travellers bring their own.
Straight roads can't shake loose
what keeps narrowing the gaze –
but they try, they track the sun.
Surrounded by your car, just
once you glimpsed him, brushed
by the moment's shine that lit you also.

The Disappeared

Montgomery Place commands
the river and much else.
Our helpful guide's precise:
"In eighteen twenty-four,
the native Americans here
disappeared". Melted
by fabrics, gilt, paint, heat,
we spill out on the lawn.

Dis-appeared. The disappeared:
how did a past participle
fade through adjective
to end up as a noun?
Strange process. As in
"wilderness" become "gardens".
The raw Catskills leap
in haze beyond a pergola.

Tight paths encircle trees
where shadows break cover,
cross lawns and shrubbery,
vanish. Trellises appear.
Borders are trim, no weeds.
What are weeds though
but displaced flowers?
It depends who –

"Disappeared", officials claim.
The rest say, "the disappeared".
Now that sun is fading
gold afternoon into dusk,
cool's ending up as chill.
Darkness is not just air.
All around are buried
verbs, the made-to-disappear.

My Brother Keeps Moving

and sometimes I catch up.
Where he had paused,
green slopes dissolved in the lake
that for now absorbed him too.
His rented house,
inch by inch, was sliding
but a hummingbird buoyed the porch.
Over our heads,
branches exchanged leaves.

Canada geese had landed.
Though they were nests
feathered by ripples, cloud
flashed just behind each eye
and they practised moonshots.
Their wakes electrified
branches not the one turtle.
A globe living in itself,
why would it need elsewhere?
The lake winked when it dived
deep among twisted roots
that were skeletons of whirlpools.

We fished later, no crossed lines.
The moon stared down
like a face which sees itself
in a mirror, the moon behind.
Where stillwater had netted
a fluster of stars, I watched
how light that fills up hours
moving boulders paints them out.
Couldn't tell water from the trees,
fell to swimming in leaves.

But Gareth kept at it, casting.
Soon he'd be off, another trip home.
And I recalled the hummingbird:
as if from a sprinkler,
one droplet had slipped
the common arc to spark its own,
make light of gravity, fly back
to feed on where it came from.

Between flight and stillness,
hovering, he raised his rod,
took aim.

Sources

Sometime I'd like to go to Crisfield, Maryland,
where "two dumb old country boys" with a barber's shop
saved themselves for other business to hand:
carved birds, imagination's airdrop

out of cleared skies. All they borrowed from was memory.
Their decoys' upswept bills, cocked heads, are records
of how life drawn to art takes off again, how teals,
canvasbacks and pintails become Wards.

Would I find things changed there on Chesapeake Bay?
You bet. What beckons though like a country road:
the illusion that where men lived is halfway
to how they saw. Which can be borrowed.

West in poet Hugo's steps years back, I tried placing
him at the Skagit, as if that darkly running song,
his secret, still floated. Cold water. Why trace
the source when a river is so long?

He'd left Port Townsend too. It was a waterspout,
flung arcs of ferries everywhere, sending –
with drops at Bremerton, Seattle – right out
to the Pacific then infinity the town's end.

To locate is to limit glittering lines of contact.
Best open yourself, not haunt abandoned yards.
Still, words are not wood. His poem "The Swimmer at..."
Sometime I'd like to see Lake Edward.

Views from the Workshed

I

Quick. A squirrel
launching the glider of its tail
flies up a trunk.

I watch what my hands
make of bandsawn wood.
Not much usually
though hands don't know that,
and anyway even our apple tree
flares only once a year.
Twisting, it can't untie its knot.

But it gives rise to birds, gives rise.
Carved birds too want to live,
blocked wings become wing blur,
heads turn to their shadows.
How to grasp what flies?

Catch, say, the dark star trilling
before it is a skylark.

II

Beyond trees: rooftopple
onto the sea murmuring
"Let's try it this way".

Shorebirds way down
at the damp edge
find windows with wandering seasons.

Even at rest, their shapes
fly through beaks
that are calling's arcs

till they disappear.
You try to follow,
taking wood, carving

liberties with the theme of S.
Shaping is all.
Finished things don't stir –

polish makes things shine,
yes, but polish seals them off.
These summer nights,

sea has a giant redwood disc
burn everything
then it's start again.

III

And another
I can't catch:
the raven of Moel Ddu
in its own sky,

that watches a path run
straight to the quarry.
Again it circles
the chapel's torn covers.

It will not follow
where streams weary
of light-splitting
idle their last laps.

It keeps, bearded, high
places. It ministers
to a quarry, lake,
a chapel that once

glimpsed souls fly up
so perfectly healed
no scars were visible.
And won't sink lower.

IV

I think of Wendell Gilley
whose eyes taking off
made sense
of what drives art to abstraction.

At Southwest Harbor, Maine,
the sea was high in branches
near the white gallery
where his birds had gathered.
I was years too late to meet him.
Didn't matter. Something
with claws, a frog-soft body
winged, the head a mallet,
had landed.
It could have swept earth's contours
through the air, beaten darkness senseless.
Bird in the wood. Wood in the bird.
Whichever way you looked at it,
his barn owl, you were looking up.

V

The Wasatch Whittlers' annual bash was packed.
"You wanna compete at the very top?"
Lance Krogue, guest speaker in a grizzled cap,
eyes clenched, hovered over us sadsacks.
"You need lessons: feathering and painting,
bird anatomy. Sharpen up – hey, look,
give it hunnert per cent. Why bet on luck?"
At that, even our braced shoulders pointed
up. Minds soared. The top called like a raven.
But you know how it is, the cosmic drag
of inertia gets in the hawk-eyed way
of thrust. Dust fell. Inspiration we flagged
at maybe ninety-five per cent, yep,
and persp- Anyway, it never added up.

VI

The sky is blank paper
I lean my mind on.

Something takes off, a flash
of desperation.
I type it anyway,
tapping at my shell,
some wordscape keen
to justify itself.

Last week a thrush
thudded against the glass.
So at least that's clear:
deception works both ways.

Outside, the yew tree
fingers splinters.
Unable to contain
its reds, it wants to break and go
whereas words are going nowhere.

I have this block of yew,
and a kestrel snatched from horizons
by my screwed-down branch
might do.

VII

Lots of ways, yes,
of getting it wrong.

Say early on
you lost proportion.

Or flaws you can't
smooth out join up.

Live into it:
things made from scratch

and scowl don't work.
How well you do

still counts when
it's what you have to do.

Symmetry's hard late on,
you get lopsided.

Overall,
carving's easier.

Ray's Birds

Lunchtime, the way he tells it,
with Ray weightless, orbiting
the forgotten planet Stress,
his chickens screech SOS
so he's off. Fox?
No, they're spun shuttlecocks
because just yards away
stands a peregrine on a jay
quivering, spread to take the spike.
Ray drifts dreamlike.
When the falcon lifts and its full load
drags it down, he lunges, rolls
to save the jay, jaycrazy,
grabs a leg. And sits up. Dazed,
he's got the falcon. Flared eyes
flash beak. Ray makes – crabwise
past the pigeon loft, on wings –
for his shed, shuffles in, gets string,
gets stabbed, ties one leg to a brick towed
clattering. Leaps out. Shed explodes.

"So what now, Ray?" That's Rosalie,
unacquainted with falconry.
His arm with clenched fist
lifts. Air swoops, glory clamps his wrist
"What'll it eat?" is Ray's sole doubt,
who spends days not finding out
then tries pigeon, desperate. It's his.
For the peregrine another bloody quiz.
Chasing its eyes around, it picks
at the soft corpse, flicking
to feather it. And pecks. And tears
raw treasure – soon, compère
of the feast, Ray's killed another three.
His top racing birds look queasy.
The falcon hops on his leather glove
to stare, his lethal turtledove.

Rosalie sums up, unflinching
the whole strange thing:
"You've got to let it go".
The sky's big through that shed window,
Ray has had doubts. It's young,
so demandingly high-strung
he has no time to live in.
And he's running out of pigeon.
So he pulls the door, stands
back. Loud hoovering woodland,
an astonishment of light,
yank the fat bird right
through the cramped frame
of all that's tame
in the world of walls
out to a radiant, rayless windfall.

But Ray has wings still. Weeks later,
watching his fastest bird home straight
towards Bishop's Wood,
he'd fly too if he could.
End of a race. His timer's ready, best
time, the loft a homemade nest.
Ray's eyes
are full of sky.
Then, higher, he sees it, black
cross, black skyjack.
That falcon, tapping its wings on air
plummets, hits foursquare
his pigeon gone south
before Ray can close his mouth.
And a puff of brown
feathers filters down.
Ray's there like a praying mantis.
Don't tell him I told you this.

A Short History of the North Wales Coast

All right, agreed, just a low shelf
piled with hills. Still, it was itself –

incomprehensible come rain or war,
life folded, you'd say, in a bottom drawer –

till the railway's sudden drum
thundered "customers".

Bingo. Both sides across stunned ground
snuffled like truffle hounds.

Came a blue surge of matelots,
quaintesques, glee parties, pierrots,

and the Palace saw a real African kraal
stretch to gondolas on a canal.

St. David? Slept in magic groves a span?
Would have sold out, *Dave the Fasting Man*.

Here anyway in an early photo,
advert smart, a house on show

foreshadows what's all spick and spent.
It is the ghost of crisis present:

on her lawn like a Welcome mat,
a lady addresses a caged bird. Just that.

With the parrot though, so many
ears unlearned so much from opportunity

that tongues licked brandnew speech.
And all changed. Like that. It's teaching

time at Bagillt where our lady misrule
has started up the Parrot School.

Talacre's Big Sleep

It's January.
Bungalows, chalets hunched
in the rain are suspects.
They know it, curtained,
peering out through keyholes,
caravans too
disguised as a wall of tin.

The café dead, one car
investigates.
Up the cracked road it goes
nowhere, stops where the tide
swills dirty macs.
And back.
There are three seagulls,
two men sharing
not a lot of hair.

Any leads at the Smuggler's Inn,
that hornpipe casualty?
Around bins, nettles
shake grey heads.

Back of the village,
feet up, pondering,
dunes slump on one another.
Gimme a light,
says the lighthouse.
The arcade without electric
schlock treatments
is not amused.

And you are the witness,
drawn again to the scene
of your own making.
What can you say,
"Arrest the rain"?

NEW POEMS

The Truth

So our local writing tutor
is offering to dig out
(it says here) "the potential
lying" in everyone. Just
what we need, more liars.

Danny's fit, he says,
after "rigorous workouts".
He's a step from rigor mortis.
And though our vicar talks community,
dentists get closer, poke
in your mouth, swap breath,
sex for the rigid frigid.
Around here, virtual reality
they were virtually born to.

Try wearing a cheery trailblazer
with eyes bloodshot, outnumbered
in a skirmish with some scotch.
You'll always walk alone.
Phil the landlord of the Anchor
barks at the emptiness:
"Should have been here lunchtime!"

You don't need a play to see
how people with one wall missing
act. Look at Arthur scaling
the south face of his barstool.
"How's the painting?" he asks.
I want to paint. But
the hermit way up on my northern
slopes has joined a ski club.

Mr. Jones

Celebs have to keep
their glamour hoists
so strenuously well-oiled
you could creak for them.
Try though getting sympathy
in a small town.
"Too close to be friends,"
sigh rapture and rupture.

Think of Mr. Jones,
leaving clothes, shoes,
debts, in the usual neat pile
who took an overdose of sea
apparently. A bachelor,
a beach: life had led him

but truth is
sea hadn't let him down.
Police kept an open eye.
The tide had been going out –
unlike his footprints
en route to anywhere,
stealing back up the sand.

Sleep-walking, he claimed.
You think he got sympathy?
This is a quiet place
tough for sleep-walkers
since nobody sees the problem.

Ol' Man River

When the light goes, night's muzzle
with silencer points straight at us
so we grab tv.

Mr. N – seemed wedded
to prim standards. Days
couldn't tell each other apart,
the cat devouring itself,
lips going lickety-split.
Night-time when minds go
walkabout was a different matter.
For his habit
of "trying car door handles",
he was fined £30 and bound in rumour.

It's true: tv will leave you
to get a life
if you don't watch it.

Tiptoeing along the coast,
dowsing for trouble,
the local newspaper serves our need
for things familiar yet mysterious,
a sandpiper tripping the sea.

The flood though will keep
rushing in.
Hearing 'Ol' Man River'
("tired of living and scared of dying")
alarmed my child who asked
"What's he going to do then?"
Lots of things, lots.
But when coffee's a kidney punch
and taps sizzling suggest
a piss, life must get....

Best give thought short boundaries.
With someone at an airport once,
"Those men," I opined
as they shoved pipes into the plane,
"have our lives in their hands".
"Right," he said.
"They're cleaning out the shit."

Revival

Grey with their burdens,
chapels like elephants remember
the Word.
It's fading to 'extinction'.
There'd better be a new word
soon
say detox desperadoes
undercover at Kwik-Save tills.

Replies the garden centre: 'conifers'.
Near our patron Sainsbury,
for all sick of lonesome pining
there's cider with rosé.

It is not enough.
The middle-aged stir in their skins.
What they belong to claimed
their youth, it never claimed to last,
and they aren't impressed
by drugs like lit piers stalking out
to make the dark disappear.

But sex lasts.
Unclothed beneath their clothes,
they aren't waiting for the off.
They leave families bug-eyed,
bounce to exits marked
Divorce on heat-seeking missions
all over town,
inflatables passion has swelled.

It's millennium fever rife.
Sex is body's answer to the mind's
"Where will I be when...?"
Phones sound mating calls,
taxis ricochet.
                    "Not here."

Blame Walt

Dead-eyed, the critics
gave our operatic society's
merry widows the waltz-over
but what do they know?
I blame Walt
for raising expectations.

It's not the dancing, it's
the dance for all of us – loose
fitters, car boot voyeurs,
shopkeepers praying summer
will bury their winter dead,
our yachtsman even in fat white
sweater like a macramé octopus –
who do not dance ourselves.

Let soaps rinse brains
for the next episode. Let walls
crowd the same picture hanging
on. For one week, even
on refugees from Albanian
theme bars, hung over
like lemurs, music pours
as from a lawn spraying
hosepipe hosannas.

If dreaming were water,
this would be Venice.

Things Upside-down

Slate roofs ripple, loose scales
of ancient fish. Loftily still,
EMPORIUM stares down the tourist trade.
Stained glass flecks upper shopfronts.
Beneath, all's brand new –
the high street's an archeological dig
upside-down.

So what?
It has taken a lifetime, failing
to answer that. But today I was listening
to the golf club's venerable bede
in deerstalker sprung from some bank
or brae, wondering why buck teeth
and earnestness go together
like a horse and carriage, when I saw
two Mormon missionaries argue furiously.
And understood at least
something upside-down, I wasn't born
again yesterday.

I know too why our tourism chief
sends crowds the wrong way:
so yachtsmen, pigeon fanciers
and mysterious old dykes
at the edge of town can go unmolested.

Hard to grasp though
is how/why bureaucracy moved in.
Fax facts: the hospital's documented
out, the high school a paper mill.
Teachers rustle. Some kids
get blown away, high fliers,
others are cracks papered over.
Inspectors approve, of course,
paper tigers. But a hurricane
could set back education hereabouts
oh, three miles or more.

Last week jet skiers, fairground
escapees, under spray cover,
buzzed yachts, bombilated, made waves
fireworks. Marvellous, just tore
up everything.
Except – that puts paid
to our tourism master plan.

Native Returns

We're coastal but fishing boats
don't fidget or ropes rap masts.
At the pub with ship's rigging
around portholes, pure art-decko,
an accordionist's smile
has the squeeze put on it
as he tries to race his fingers.

Ron's dad is not impressed.

We show him the pond
where, heads down, hands pocketed,
moorhens still scurry.
Wind in Bishop's Wood
does rough carpentry.
He meets a man with memories,
with jowls like a pelican's.

Nothing.
Returned after fifty years,
he recalls a lighthouse like an island,
and flags on the Lido,
red-yellow gas lamps flickering.

On a crystal night,
we three are looking out to sea.
To the west, the island
has returned with its rare
promise: a new start freshened
by thirty miles of sea.
And, east, a galleon on fire –
masts flying the horizon's
pennant – does not go down.
It seems an eternal flame.
It is an oil-rig.

The old man stares and stares.

Application for a Canal

Winter. The town takes
to its armchair
against a sea of troubles.

June and the main road's
everywhere, scoops up
people it hasn't dumped yet,
circling their holidays.
Visitors bring fever.
We keep
calm but cannot keep it safe.

The place needs a canal
to show that just lying
there is another way to go,
how ripples come and
come without making waves
as roofs fall in with sky.
A new slant, that's all,
to be opposite of roads.

So you'd glance down,
say, into a fountain of green
coins – that branches catch
and light counts underwater.

Acknowledgements

Amongst other magazines, some of these poems have appeared in *Cumberland Poetry Review, Lines Review, Literature and Belief, New Mexico Humanities Review, New Welsh Review, North Dakota Quarterly, Oxford Poetry, Planet, Poetry Wales, South Dakota Review, Stand*, and *Tar River Poetry*. The anthologies in which some of these poems have appeared include: *A Book of Wales* (Dent), *Anglo-Welsh Poetry 1480-1980* (Poetry Wales Press), *Harvest* (Salt Lake City), *The Bright Field* (Carcanet), *The Critical Eye* (Texas), *The Urgency of Identity* (Chicago), *Twentieth-Century Anglo-Welsh Poetry* (Seren), *Wales: an Anthology* (Collins), *Wales in Verse* (Secker & Warburg). Some poems have been heard on BBC Radio Wales, BBC Radio 4 and on BBC Television.

In Washington, 'Taking the Mail to Walla Walla' was published as a broadsheet by Stanza Press; 'Salmon' appeared in *Chambers Creek Cantata* (Steelhead Press) and other poems in *Janus Rising* (Vardaman Press). Included in the poem 'From Kelly's Diary' are extracts from *We Were Not Summer Soldiers* (Washing State Historical Society, 1976), the Indian War Diary of Plympton J. Kelly, 1855-56.

Original poems in their own right, the sonnets in the sequence 'Reading the Country' were prompted partly by poems translated from the Welsh, whose titles have been retained. The translations were found in *The Poetry of Wales 1930-1970* by R. Gerallt Jones (1970) and *Twentieth Century Welsh Poems* by Joseph Clancy (1982). The poets are:

I.	T. Glynne Davies	VIII.	T.H. Parry-Williams
II.	Iorwerth C. Peate	IX.	R. Williams Parry
III.	Gwyn Thomas	X.	Waldo Williams
IV.	Gwyn Thomas	XI.	Waldo Williams
V.	Gwynne Williams	II.	Gwynn Jones
VI.	W.J. Gruffydd	XIII.	T.H. Parry-Williams
VII.	Gwilym R. Jones	XIV.	Euros Bowen

These poems are selected from:

At the Edge of Town (Gomer Press, 1981)
The Silence in the Park (Poetry Wales Press, 1982)
The Visitor's Book (Seren, 1985)
Flight Patterns (Seren, 1991)
Dirt Roads (Seren, 1997)